T0245029

It Won't Ever Be the Same

A TEEN'S GUIDE TO GRIEF AND GRIEVING

Korie Leigh, Ph.D.
with contributions from teens

Library of Congress Cataloging-in-Publication Data
Names: Leigh, Korie, author.
Title: It won't ever be the same : a teen's guide to grief and grieving / Korie Leigh, Ph.D., with
    contributions from teens.
Other titles: It will not ever be the same
Description: Minneapolis, MN : Free Spirit Publishing, an imprint of Teacher Created Materials,
    [2024] | Includes index. | Audience: Ages 11+
Identifiers: LCCN 2024013207 (print) | LCCN 2024013208 (ebook) | ISBN 9798885543842 (paperback) |
    ISBN 9798885543859 (ebook) | ISBN 9798885543866 (epub)
Subjects: LCSH: Grief in adolescence--Juvenile literature. | Loss (Psychology) in adolescence--Juvenile
    literature. | Teenagers and death--Juvenile literature. | BISAC: YOUNG ADULT NONFICTION /
    Social Topics / Death, Grief, Bereavement | YOUNG ADULT NONFICTION / Health & Daily Living /
    Mental Health
Classification: LCC BF724.3.G73 L45 2024 (print) | LCC BF724.3.G73 (ebook) | DDC
    155.9/370835--dc23/eng/20240424
LC record available at https://lccn.loc.gov/2024013207
LC ebook record available at https://lccn.loc.gov/2024013208

Edited by Cassie Labriola-Sitzman
Cover and interior design by Michelle Lee Lagerroos
Words and artwork by teens are used with permission.

Printed by: 70548
Printed in: China
PO#: 12369

Free Spirit Publishing
An imprint of Teacher Created Materials
9850 51st Avenue North, Suite 100
Minneapolis, MN 55442
(612) 338-2068
help4kids@freespirit.com
freespirit.com

For all the teens who allowed me to walk alongside them in their grief and the families who trusted me to witness and hold their grief. And for all the colleagues who taught me, mentored me, and believed in my vision.

Contents

Introduction

"It's like when you break something into a million pieces.

You know how you try to put it back together?

Even though most of the pieces are there,

there are just as many that are missing.

You'll never find them again.

You can sort of put it back together,

but it won't ever look the same."

These words were shared by a 13-year-old whose dad had died, in an attempt to explain the way grief felt to them.

1

Grief is a universal human experience—every person will grieve at some point in their life. You're reading this book because you're grieving right now, and that can be really hard.

Grief often feels isolating and confusing. The people in your life might not know what to say or do, or they may say and do the wrong things. They may treat you differently than before. Or they might be grieving so much themselves that they don't recognize your grief at all.

Maybe you picked up this book because you want some support in your grief. Or maybe you want to hear about what other teens have experienced in their own grieving processes. Whatever the reason, this book is written for you—to help you feel less alone and more connected, to teach you new ways of understanding yourself and your grief, and to help you make sense of the difficult experience you're going through.

About This Book

Whether you are in the midst of your first grief experience, have been grieving a while, or have experienced grief many times before, this book is designed to support you. No matter how long you've been grieving, it can be helpful to express your grief in new ways. The activities, reflections, and analogies within these pages guide you in working through your personal and complex grief experience.

Throughout the book, you will also meet other teens who have experienced big losses. These young people have shared their words and artwork with me, and they have given me permission to share them with you. Some wanted to give their names and more details about their grief, while others wanted to remain anonymous and keep the details of their grief more private. A few, including Ray, Sofia, Jonah, Jaida, and Amelie, share their voices and stories multiple times.

These words and art pieces help you understand other teens' experiences with grief, what grief has felt like for them, and how they've coped with it. Most of all, I hope that reading about these teens' experiences helps you find the words and images to express your grief and know that you are never alone.

Here are a few more things to know as you read.

Each section starts with an analogy about grief, followed by artwork or words from grieving teens. The analogies come from a poem I wrote about grief when I first started creating this book. You can find the full poem on pages 124–128. Here are other recurring features you'll find.

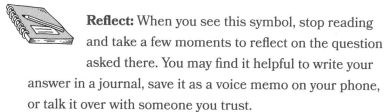

Reflect: When you see this symbol, stop reading and take a few moments to reflect on the question asked there. You may find it helpful to write your answer in a journal, save it as a voice memo on your phone, or talk it over with someone you trust.

Give It a Try: When you see this symbol, put down the book and try out the process, idea, or activity described there. You might do these activities with someone you trust, or you can do them on your own.

Intention: These moments invite you to consider or try out a new way of being in the world. They require you to be intentional in what you are thinking, doing, or saying in your day-to-day life.

Feel: When you see this symbol, take a moment to tune into your emotions and explore how you feel.

How to Use This Book

I suggest starting at the beginning of the book and making your way through it. It will take a while to work through all the activities—it's okay to put the book down and come back to it after some time, whether that break is a few days or weeks. You can also jump to the section that sounds most like where you are, right now, in your grief. The sections are divided into parts that touch upon big milestones in the grief journey, starting with new grief and continuing through the days, weeks, months, and years after.

However you choose to make your way through the book, use the text as a guide to explore your grief. The prompts and activities can help you to put into words the wordless, visualize the shapeless, and describe this utterly complex experience. Do all of them as you read, or read them first and then choose the ones that feel right for you. You can also come back to these words and activities and do them multiple times.

Some teens like to talk through the prompts or do the activities with a counselor, some like to do them with other young people who are grieving, and some like to do them completely on their own. There is no right or wrong way, but it can be helpful to keep everything you create so you can reflect on your grief and see how it changes over time. A special journal or binder is a wonderful tool for keeping your writing and art all in one place.

It Won't Ever Be the Same

Look again at the quote that starts this introduction. Do these words sound like your grief? Maybe they do, or they might not sound like your grief at all. A different quote in these pages might feel more like your experience. The analogies that start each chapter may help you in writing your own analogies about your grief (see page 28). Grief can be very difficult to describe and explain. It's messy and complicated. It likely feels overwhelming and intense, at least some of the time. And it changes over time.

Your grief is your own and only you know what it feels like. I hope the following pages help you name, express, and give shape to your grief so that you may learn to understand it.

PART I

What Is Grief?

Exploring Grief

Someone has died; Someone is forever gone.
Something has been lost; Something has been found.
Something terrible has happened.

—Anonymous, age 15

Grief is something that every single person on Earth feels at some point in their life. Some experience grief for the first time as little kids; others first experience it when they are teenagers. Some people don't experience grief until much later in life.

Lots of people experience grief for the first time when a person or animal close to them dies. But grief isn't felt only when someone dies. People might feel grief after a divorce in their family or another big family change. They might feel grief when they move away from friends and family, when they see the impact of climate change on the planet, or when they or someone close to them receives life-altering news, like a serious medical diagnosis. People feel grief for a lot of reasons that have nothing to do with a death.

So, what *is* grief? Grief is unique to each person, which makes it hard to find just one way to describe it.

A good way to think about grief is as *the way you respond to a loss*. That's still pretty broad, so let's break it down. You *respond* to loss not just one way, but many ways, often happening all at once. Here are a few of the ways you might respond.

Emotional: Experiencing a loss triggers an emotional reaction. For some, that may mean tears, crying, and sadness. For others, it could be disbelief, numbness, or shock. Some might feel anger, guilt, or hopelessness. All these emotions are normal responses to a loss, and you may experience them at different times throughout the days, weeks, and years following the loss.

Emotions also impact how you feel physically in your body and can influence how you feel about yourself and how you move through the world and interact with friends, family, and other people in your life.

Physical: The body also grieves after a loss. You may feel physically weak or in pain. Your joints may hurt, food may taste different, or it may feel like you have bricks or weights in your legs. You may sleep a lot more, or a lot less.

Relationship with yourself: When someone you love dies, it can feel like you don't know yourself anymore. The things you used to enjoy might not be fun any longer; the way you used to talk or wear clothes might not feel right. You may even have big questions about your purpose in life.

Relationships with others: Loss can have a big impact on your relationships. The loss might be a person with whom you had a relationship, or it may impact other relationships in your life. Friends, teachers, and family members may treat you differently. People at school may say hurtful things. You may not want to participate in group activities, sports, or hobbies that you used to like.

Thinking: Your brain grieves too. People who have experienced loss will talk about how, right after the loss, their brains felt sluggish. You may find that you think more slowly, have trouble concentrating, are more forgetful, or feel foggy. A loss can also affect the kind of thoughts you have. Maybe it makes you rethink who you are and what you want to do, or maybe it changes how you view the world and your position in it.

Spiritual: Whether you are religious or not, after a loss, you may experience changes in your faith or spiritual beliefs. You may find you start asking hard questions like these: *What is my purpose in life? Why is there so much pain in life? Why do bad things happen to kind people?*

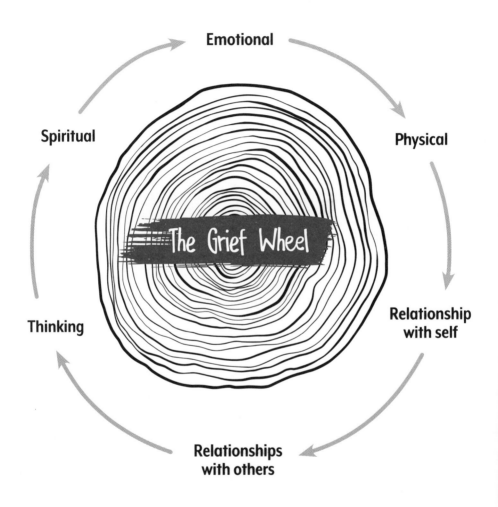

Emotional

Spiritual

Physical

Thinking

Relationship
with self

Relationships
with others

The Grief Wheel

As the grief wheel illustrates, a loss affects your *entire self.* You feel grief emotionally, act it out in your body, relate to the people around you differently, understand yourself differently, and may develop new beliefs or shed old ones. Some areas of your grief wheel may feel fuller than others. For example, maybe you're feeling emotionally overwhelmed, but not experiencing many physical effects. Or maybe you're questioning your relationships to yourself and others, but your spiritual beliefs have stayed mostly the same. That's okay. The areas that feel most full may change from day to day, and year to year, as your grief changes.

REFLECT

Which areas of your grief wheel feel really full right now? Which feel emptier?

Grief is the way you respond to a loss. And you can feel loss for anything that is meaningful in your life. When you lose a person, that loss might mean that the person died. But loss also happens when people don't die.

You can feel loss whenever someone you care about is separated from you, by distance or another issue. This separation might be from incarceration, deployment, substance use or abuse, placement into foster care, the person being missing, one of you moving away, or mental health issues. The term for this kind of loss is *ambiguous loss*. These losses are sometimes harder to describe because you often don't get a sense of closure with them. The person is still living, but you don't see them or interact with them in the way you did before.

Losses can also occur within yourself. You can lose part of your identity, your sense of belonging, your sense of safety in the world, trust in your body, or a sense of who you are.

You might also experience *intergenerational losses*. These are losses that your parents, grandparents, or great grandparents experienced that are still affecting your family. These kinds of losses are not always talked about openly. They might include escaping one's home country and becoming a refugee; experiencing persecution for a religious, ethnic, or cultural identity; or experiences of war.

Another kind of grief that many people experience is from *anticipatory loss*. Anticipatory losses are ones that we know are coming, and though they haven't yet transpired, we still grieve for what we know is going to happen. For example, maybe someone has a terminal illness and you know they will die, but they haven't yet. Or you have a grandparent who is aging, and you can see their physical decline, but their mental abilities are still intact.

The tricky thing about grief is that the way you respond to a loss may not be the same with each loss you experience. When someone you love dies, you might respond to that loss in a different way than how you'd respond if you move away from your friends and school. Likewise, the relationship you had with the person may mean you grieve differently. For example, if a parent dies, your grief may look and feel different than if a classmate dies. Maybe there will be some similarities, but there will likely be a lot of differences too.

All losses are hard to cope with and understand. While the majority of this book focuses on grief due to the death of a person, you can apply the concepts and approaches to any loss you are grieving.

REFLECT

Take a look at the grief wheel again and think about the ways you've responded to the losses in your life. What do you notice? What are the similarities? What are the differences?

Loss Lines

A loss line is a visual representation of all the losses, big and small, that you've experienced throughout your life. Viewing your losses like this can help you remember that you've made it through tough times before. A loss line also helps you see the ways that all people have experienced grief and is especially helpful to return to in times when you're feeling alone in your grief.

Instructions

1. Take a piece of paper and draw a line across it.

2. Label one end of the line "before I was born." Label the other end "today," and date it.

3. Think about the losses in your life, big and small, tangible and intangible, from however far back you can remember. Then begin to add them to your line. Label these losses in any way you want. Remember

to include *all* losses: moving houses, a pet dying, a relationship ending, a person dying, and any intergenerational losses in your family.

4. When you are done, flip to a clean sheet of paper or open a composition app on your computer or phone (anything that gives you a space to write).

5. Set a timer for three minutes, and write as much as possible about your loss line. You can use the following prompts to help you get started, but you don't need to write about any specific prompt.

   - When I look at my loss line, the emotions I feel are . . .

   - When I look at my loss line, I realize . . .

   - When I look at my loss line, some questions I have are . . .

6. When you finish writing, read what you've written. And share what you discovered with someone you trust. Sharing your experiences with someone can help you better understand your grief and feel less alone in it.

Describing Your Grief

Grief is like a messy, complex, layered
All or nothing, small or large
Ball of yarn

"Grief is masking and thinking and trying
to make sure everyone else around you is okay
you lose who you are and what you love
but it's okay because
nothing will ever be the same anyway"

—Jaida, age 14

23

Grief is complicated and complex. It's not just one thing. In fact, if you were to ask one hundred people what grief is, you would probably get one hundred unique answers.

Here's how Amelie defines grief:

"Grief is like that analogy of a box with a ball and a pain button in it. At the beginning, the ball is huge, and, therefore, the pain button gets pressed more often than not. But as the months and years go on, the ball shrinks. It doesn't happen overnight. Rather, it's a slow and tedious process. But when the ball doesn't hit the pain button as often, we might forget it's there altogether. We might even think we've beaten it. But eventually it presses the button again, and we notice it more when it does. It is something that our brains try to push into the back of our minds. But it demands to be heard and processed.

"Like a ball of string, grief is like a loose thread that untangles the whole ball. When you try to put it back together again, it is never quite the same. A part of you was taken out."

−Amelie, age 16

Sofia describes her grief in an entirely different way:

"I would envision grief as a person who's curled up in a ball, not talking to anyone. When I first experienced loss, I didn't know who I could talk to. I had no friends in the same situation, so I became reserved. However, I would also describe grief as something/someone sporadic. I imagine the person sitting across from me to have red puffy eyes from crying, probably tired from the countless nights thinking about the loss."

The earliest known uses of the word *grief* as we know it in the English language come from the thirteenth century, where it meant "physical hardship, suffering, or pain." The more modern use of the word dates to the fourteenth century. The Latin origin of the English word *grieve* is *gravare*, meaning "to burden or make heavy."

Around the globe, there are many languages that do not have a word for grief, which makes sense. It is very hard to distill the experience of grief into a single word. For example, the French word *la douleur* can be used to mean "pain," "sorrow," "ache," or "grief." And the Farsi *ænduh* expresses "grief" and "regret." Grief goes by many names and means something different in each language, culture, family, and religion.

REFLECT

If you were to create your own word for grief, what would it be?

INTENTION

Do you ever feel too alone in your grief? In many places around the world, people have long understood grief as a collective experience. Hindus, the Lakota and other Indigenous peoples, as well as Buddhists and many Chinese families are among the communities that practice collective grief. Rather than leaving the griever alone, family, friends, and neighbors come together to provide food, community, and ritual to ease emotional pain.

Ask people in your family or community how they would describe and define grief. What beliefs do people in your culture or religion have about it? What rituals or practices are there to support the griever? How would you like to be with others in your grief?

One of the hardest parts about describing your grief is trying to make sense out of an experience that is utterly senseless. But when something huge and hard-to-understand happens, there are helpful strategies you can try to make the

INTENTION

If you were to define grief, what would you say? How would you describe such a big and complex experience?

event more understandable. One of the best is to describe the experience itself, as Jaida, Amelie, and Sofia have done. This might sound a bit weird, but give it a try and see what happens.

Defining big and complex experiences like grief can be very difficult. Using analogy puts a hard-to-understand experience into words that help you make sense of it. If you were to define grief using an analogy, what would you say? If you're having trouble getting started, flip to page 124 and use one of those analogies as a jumping-off point for writing your own. Or try thinking through the following prompt as a way to get started.

Right now, in your grief, what are you experiencing?

- crying or not crying

- numbness or overwhelm

- wanting to be alone or wanting to be around others

- wanting to talk about your loved one or not wanting to talk about them

- talking to your loved one out loud or in your head or not talking to them at all

- finding little moments that make you feel connected to your loved one or finding ways to disconnect and distance yourself from them

- feeling guilty or like the person's death was your fault or forgiving yourself for whatever you might regret

Another way to describe grief is to use art to create a visual representation of it. Whether you use words or images or a mixture of both, finding ways to describe your grief experience can help you better understand what your grief feels like. Often grief is so messy and complex that it is hard to know exactly how you feel. By using color, shape, and texture to visualize your grief, you might find it easier to describe.

What Does Your Grief Look Like?

Using images, words, color, and texture, create a visual representation of your grief. This can be done with only a few art materials or with lots of materials. And it can take as short or long a time as you'd like, depending on how in-depth you want to go. This activity is one I do with a lot of teens, and it can help you describe your specific grief experience.

Instructions:

1. Gather a few pieces of multimedia art paper (or any paper thicker than regular printer paper) and various art materials. Then follow the prompts below. Use a new sheet of paper for each prompt.

   • Describe your grief using colors. Look at your color options and choose only the colors that you feel represent your grief. Use just those colors to fill one entire sheet of paper.

- Using the same colors you used in the previous prompt, describe your grief by focusing on its shape and size. How big does it feel from one day to the next? Create this image on a new sheet of paper.

- On another new sheet of paper, describe your grief as if it were a person. Imagine your grief is sitting in a chair across from you. What do you see?

- Finally, describe your grief using only adjectives. Fill an entire sheet of paper with these adjectives, use them to create a design, or do whatever feels right to you.

2. Display your images so you can see them all at once. Take your time and look over each one by itself. Now look at them all together as a group.

3. Set a timer for three minutes. On a new sheet of paper or in a composition app, write whatever comes to mind about the images you created. You might write about what you noticed in the images, or write about what thoughts, feelings, or memories they evoke.

PART II
Feeling Grief

Immediate Aftermath

My world has been shattered. Turned upside down.
Broken and scattered.

The love I had now makes way for grief.

Grief is like the everlasting shape of that love.

"Grief is like a loss that can't be stopped."

—Jonah, age 14

Someone you love or care about died. The news of their death may have been sudden and shocking. It might also have been something you were expecting if the person was very sick or was dealing with a terminal illness. Whether the news was shocking or expected, it likely left you feeling numb, scared, confused, or all these emotions at the same time. When you first heard, you may have felt as if you were living on some other weird planet, walking through a fog, or running a marathon with cement legs. You might have wanted to scream or drop to your knees and sob. You might have felt a sense of relief, especially if the person was sick for a long time. Or maybe you felt nothing at all, an emptiness.

This is what Ray shares about learning their dad died by suicide.

"My dad died in July 2016, from suicide. I was at my grand-parents' house when it happened. We had a family meeting a few days after, and my mom and grandma broke the news to me and my brother, who was only five at the time. I remember thinking of all the horrible things that could have happened. I was looking around the room and noticed my dad was the only one who wasn't in the room. Then the most shattering words came out of my mom's mouth. 'Daddy's gone.' I don't remember crying, to be honest. Just sort of taking it in, like it hadn't hit me yet. It did hit me, eventually, like a train."

Maybe you feel guilt for not acting a certain way after hearing that the person died. Some people don't cry and then feel guilty for not crying. Others cry a lot and feel guilty for

 **FEEL**

Place one hand on your chest and the other on your stomach. Gently breathe, so that your hands on your stomach and chest rise and fall with your breath. Breathe in through your nose. Slowly blow your breath out through your mouth. Try to name the emotions you feel at this very moment.

crying too much. I know it can be hard, but try to accept whatever your initial emotional response was. In that moment, it was right for you. It was a normal way for your brain to make sense of something shocking and terrible.

In fact, your emotional responses actually start in your brain. Your brain can roughly be divided into three parts: the body brain, the feeling brain, and the thinking brain.

Body brain—this part of the brain operates 24/7, all on its own. It's how you breathe, how you digest food, and how your heart beats.

Thinking brain—this part helps you plan, think, problem-solve, and multitask. It also helps you understand language and coordinates your whole body so you can walk, talk, listen to music, and chew gum at the same time.

Feeling brain—this part controls your emotional responses, including your response to stress. Some people call this the limbic brain, or the fight-or-flight part of the brain. It works to create an emotional experience that you have in your body and your mind.

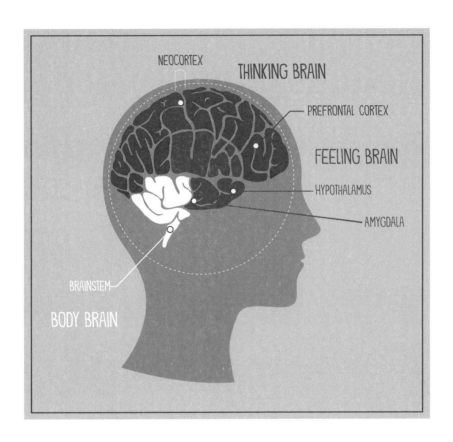

NEOCORTEX

THINKING BRAIN

— PREFRONTAL CORTEX

FEELING BRAIN

HYPOTHALAMUS

AMYGDALA

BRAINSTEM

BODY BRAIN

However you felt when you first heard the news was your brain's way of protecting itself from the shock of that news. Your body brain, thinking brain, and feeling brain were working together to cause your response. Then your feeling brain took over and sent you in one of a few ways:

- **Freeze**—Freezing looks like feeling numb or empty. If your brain caused you to freeze, you may not have had much of an emotional response.

- **Fight**—The fight response can look like an outburst of emotions, anger, sadness, or disbelief. Fight makes sure these emotions are expressed. You may cry, or scream, or not believe the news.

- **Flight**—The flight, or run away, response can look like literally running away from the person telling you the terrible news. It can also look like trying to distract yourself from thinking about the event, or filling every moment of your day with something to do so that you don't have time to focus on the loss.

- **Fawn**—The fawn response can look like immediately going into caretaking mode. You are more concerned about those around you: How are *they* feeling? Are *they* okay? You focus all your attention, energy, and emotions on ensuring those around you are taken care of.

Your brain has a built-in system, sort of like a piece of software code. That code tells you what to do when you experience something shocking or scary or become overwhelmed. And it's what causes you to have a freeze, fight, flight, or fawn response. In those moments, your emotional and physical reactions are not a choice.

Thinking about when you heard the news that your loved one had died may bring up many of the same feelings and overwhelm of those moments. Even though you didn't get to choose your initial response, you can calm the overwhelm you might feel at the memories. Breathing (page 42) is one of the simplest ways to do this, and you can use it anywhere and anytime you are feeling overwhelmed. Paying attention to your senses (page 58) is another strategy that helps get your body and brain into a more relaxed state.

It's normal to experience overwhelm, especially in the first weeks and months of your grief. As your grief transforms over time, you will learn ways to cope with the overwhelm.

4/2/6 Breathing

One way to help calm your overwhelm is a specific type of breathing called the 4/2/6 breath.

Instructions

1. When you notice you are feeling overwhelmed, breathe in through your nose as you count slowly to four.

2. Hold your breath as you count to two.

3. Breathe out through your mouth to the count of six.

4. Repeat this pattern for as many breaths as you need.

5. Some people find using different numbers more helpful, such as 5/3/7 breathing or 3/2/5 breathing. Use whatever number count works best for you. What's most important is that you breathe out longer than you breathe in.

Grounding with Ice

Another technique that can be helpful when you're feeling overwhelmed is called grounding with ice. This strategy might sound strange, but give it a try if you need support when you are feeling emotionally overwhelmed or are in the middle of an intense grief burst.

Instructions

1. Find a freezer and get an ice cube. If there are no ice cubes, grab any other frozen item.

2. Hold the ice cube in one hand while using 4/2/6 breathing.

3. Focus on your 4/2/6 breaths and notice the sensation of the cold ice in your hand.

4. Do this for three to five breaths and then check in with your body. Notice if your overwhelm has shifted in any way.

Grief in the Body

Grief is like a pounding in the chest,
an aching in the muscles,
and a breaking of the heart.
Why do I feel so tired all the time?

—Jaida, age 14

IT WON'T EVER BE THE SAME

One thing about grief that is often not talked about is how it is experienced and felt in the body. Recall the physical piece of the grief wheel from page 16. Grief is not just how you respond emotionally to a loss; it's also how your body responds.

Think about how you feel emotions in your body. When you are embarrassed, your cheeks may flush and turn red; when you're around someone you like a lot, your stomach might feel as if it is full of butterflies. When you get angry, your hands and face might feel hot. Since grief is such a complex and emotional experience, it's no wonder that you experience it in your body too.

Ray shares how grief feels in their body:

"Ever since my dad's death, I have had a lot of physical issues. Stomachaches, body tremors, and headaches too."

Here are some other common ways that grief shows up in the body:

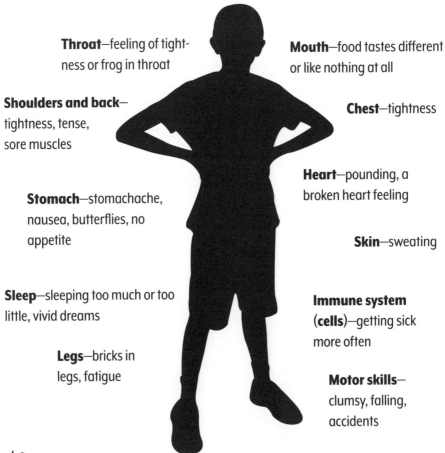

Head—headaches, confusion, brain fog

Throat—feeling of tightness or frog in throat

Mouth—food tastes different or like nothing at all

Shoulders and back—tightness, tense, sore muscles

Chest—tightness

Stomach—stomachache, nausea, butterflies, no appetite

Heart—pounding, a broken heart feeling

Skin—sweating

Sleep—sleeping too much or too little, vivid dreams

Immune system (cells)—getting sick more often

Legs—bricks in legs, fatigue

Motor skills—clumsy, falling, accidents

Feeling your grief in your body is normal. It is a natural part of the grieving process, and everyone experiences it to different degrees. Identifying the ways grief shows up in your body is a very helpful approach to understanding why you're feeling a certain way. And sharing these body symptoms with others can help them better understand your needs.

REFLECT

Look at the body outline. What would you add to this list that you have experienced? What would you cross off?

GIVE IT A TRY

Body Mapping

Body mapping can help you identify where in your body you feel grief. You might even try doing this activity with a trusted adult to help them better understand your grief.

Instructions

1. Draw a simple outline of a body.

2. Using color, fill in the parts of the body outline where you experience your grief.

3. You could also do this activity as a collage, cutting out images, words, and colors and pasting them on the parts of the body outline where you feel grief.

4. If you'd like to, find a trusted adult and share your collage with them. Explore together what you learned about your grief.

Grief Brain

Grief is like walking through a thick fog; but the fog is in my brain.

"Grief is like forgetting how to read and not being able to do my homework."

–Jonah, age 14

51

Has your grief ever had you feeling like you are walking through a fog? Or like your thoughts are all scrambled together? If so, you are not alone. In fact, there is a name for this kind of experience: *grief brain*.

When you are grieving, some parts of your brain are more activated than others. This can lead to a sense of foggy-headedness. If you have grief brain, you might:

- forget things

- have thoughts that are jumbled together

- feel as if you're moving in slow motion when everyone else is moving in real time

- be clumsier, fall over things, and trip more often

These effects are all due to your brain trying to relearn the world. The loss of a person literally changes your brain, temporarily. It's normal to feel off balance, or forgetful, or like you can't possibly do your homework or study for a test.

Know that the fog will get better. It will change, just as you do.

Brain Release

If you feel like brain fog is affecting your ability to focus, remember, complete homework, or do other things that you want or need to do, try this activity.

Instructions

1. Find a comfortable place to either lie down or sit. Make sure the place is quiet and free of distractions.

2. Some people like to have ambient sound or white noise in the background when they are doing a brain release. But you don't have to. You can do this activity in complete silence too.

3. Now, rate on a scale of 1 to 10 how much stress your body is holding in this moment.

4. To start your brain release, imagine you are squeezing your brain like you would your bicep or abdominal muscles. Imagine squeezing your brain as hard as you can.

5. Now, focus on relaxing your brain. Release every part and every muscle around your head, your eyes, your ears, your neck—even your hair.

6. Repeat squeezing and releasing your brain three times.

7. Rate on a scale of 1 to 10 how much stress your body is holding after the brain release. Notice if there is any difference from when you started.

Grief Bursts

Grief is like an ocean of emotion.
Calm and smooth one moment; the next, full of motion.
A wave appears and knocks me over.

"When my brother first died, we were watching *The Sound of Music* in music class.
I noticed all the other kids were so happy.
But I couldn't be happy because my brother just died.
I started to cry in class."

–Jonah, age 14

Have you ever felt a grief burst?

Maybe there was a day when you were feeling okay and your grief didn't feel too big or too loud. Maybe you were even enjoying yourself. Then, out of the blue, an emotional tidal wave hit you. It seemed to come out of nowhere. You heard a specific song, smelled something that recalled a memory, or someone said something to you. One moment you were going along feeling okay, and the next you were crying, hyperventilating, or feeling completely overwhelmed. Thoughts, emotions, memories, sensations started to flood you.

Sound familiar?

This is a grief burst. You might hear them called them grief waves or grief attacks as well. And they are very common when people are grieving. For some, grief bursts don't seem to be triggered by anything specific. For others, something like a song, a sound, a specific date, or an interaction with a particular person can bring on a grief burst. Grief bursts happen when your grief, which is under the surface, rises up. This rising and sinking of your grief is a normal emotional process. It happens because you're feeling your pain deeply.

Grief bursts are often very intense. They may seem to come on without any warning. You might wonder if they'll ever stop or if you'll ever feel okay again. If you feel distressed, try one of the strategies you learned for dealing with overwhelm on pages 42–43. Grounding your senses (page 58) can also be helpful, as can talking to someone about your grief.

REFLECT

If you like describing things with art, try visualizing your grief burst. What does it feel like with color, shape, texture, size, and pattern? If you'd like, use art materials to create an image of your grief burst.

And remember: Grief bursts are normal. They happen to everyone, though people rarely talk about them. You are not alone.

GIVE IT A TRY

Grounding Your Senses

Grief bursts can be overwhelming, like you are back in the depths of your grief. When this happens, try focusing on your senses. This practice won't take the grief burst away entirely, but it should help you feel less overwhelmed during it.

Instructions

1. Look around your environment and name five things you see. Make them simple (the floor, your socks, the ceiling, a light, the sink).

2. Next, notice what you hear, and name four things (your own breath, people talking down the hall, a toilet flushing, a phone ringing).

3. Then, bring your awareness to what you smell. Name three things (your shampoo, the soap dispenser, lunch being cooked).

4. Now, focus on your body. Name two things you feel on your skin (your shirt on your back, the socks on your feet).

5. Next, shift your awareness to your taste. This one might be harder, but give it a try. Name one thing that you taste (your toothpaste, the last thing you ate or drank, your tears).

6. Now, as a final step, notice your entire body, from the top of your head to the tips of your toes. Take three deep breaths and imagine you are breathing into every cell in your body.

PART III

Making Meaning

Creating Rituals

Grief is like holding on and letting go at the same time.
It is finding ways to remember and building new memories.

"Finding small ways to carry their memory helps the grief feel not so heavy sometimes."

—Anonymous, age 13

Losing a loved one can feel overwhelming and confusing. Finding ways to honor their memory, while also becoming the person you are without them, is complicated. There's no rule book or guide to help you do this.

One way to remember and honor your loved one is to create a ritual. Your ritual can be any act that you do that has intention, meaning, or purpose. Whatever it is, it should be a sacred and special act that helps you feel connected to your loved one. A ritual can be a small thing that you think or feel, like when a specific song comes on and you take a moment to think of the person, or something bigger that you do or create, like planting and caring for a tree or making a memory collage.

When thinking about how to start a ritual, it might be helpful to ask yourself, *How do I want to remember my loved one? What does remembering look like to me?* The following list offers ideas you might want to try.

- Make memorial jewelry or something that you can wear every day to remind you of the person.

- Find a special place in nature that reminds you of them and go on walks there regularly.

- Plant trees, flowers, or other plants and care for them.

- Write music about the person.

- Make art about them.

- Write poems or stories about them.

- Use their clothing to make a special item, like a quilt or stuffed animal.

Or you might want your rituals to be connected to something your loved one liked. If so, the following questions can be helpful when trying to figure out what to do.

- What did you like to do with your loved one? Do you want to continue those traditions, or do you want to make new ones?

- What was their favorite food? Would you want to serve their favorite dishes on special days or whenever you're missing them a lot?

- Do you want to spend time with other people who loved the person or be alone when doing your rituals?

- Would you want to do something in honor of them, such as volunteering with or donating to an organization or cause they cared about?

Rituals help you honor your loved one in a way that feels personal to you. But the choice is always yours. If you don't want to do anything or if a ritual doesn't feel right for you, that's okay. It may take time for you to find a way to honor your loved one that feels right.

Many rituals can be done anywhere and at any time. Some examples of these smaller rituals include an affirmation you say to yourself, a prayer, or a moment when you stop and notice how you are feeling close to or remembering your loved one.

While you don't need to wait for a special day to do your rituals, doing them on a special day can be a good way to remember and feel connected to your loved one and include their memory in your celebration or event. Lots of people like to do their rituals around holidays, special events and anniversaries, and life milestones. You can also do them any time you wish your loved one were there to celebrate with you or you want to connect with them.

Serving Others and Random Acts

Some people find that doing acts of service in memory of their loved one helps them cope with their grief. Serving others makes them feel as if they are doing something meaningful, and the simple act of *doing* can be helpful. If this sounds like something you'd be interested in, find a specific organization to volunteer with or create a fund-raiser or donation drive.

You could also create Random Acts of Kindness Cards to honor the memory of your loved one. On a special day or anniversary, give the cards to friends and family, or place them in locations that people gather, such as coffee shops or your local hangout spot. Be sure to leave these directions with your cards: "Take a card, perform a random act of kindness for a stranger, and then give that person the card." You might add a sentence on the card that the act was done in memory of your loved one.

Asking Big Questions

Grief is like learning to question,

unlearn,

and relearn the world around me.

Who am I now?

What will I become?

—Anonymous

Grief has a way of impacting the way you view and understand the world around you. Some teens have described this as looking at the world with a new pair of glasses that are perpetually foggy. When you're grieving, you may experience big questions about and changes in the way you see the world and in your religion, beliefs, and values. Asking these kinds of questions after a loss is normal, but this process can be really hard to go through on your own.

After her brother died, Sofia experienced big questions about herself. This is what she has to say about it:

"When I think of myself, grief has made me feel like a puzzle with one missing piece. When you look at it, you can tell what the picture/puzzle is supposed to look like, and you might not even notice the one missing piece. But every so often, that piece catches your eye, and you know there's something missing, but you won't ever get that piece back. I'm not trying to say that grief makes you lose part of yourself, but you know that you're forever changed once you go through a significant loss."

What are you struggling to understand right now? Here are some big questions teens have shared with me. Maybe you are asking some of these questions too.

- Why did they die?

- Was it my fault?

- How can the world be so cruel?

- Why do bad things happen to good people?

- Who am I now that my loved one has died?

REFLECT

What are some questions you have been dealing with since your loved one died? In what ways do you feel like you are having to relearn the world around you? What does your puzzle look like?

Asking these kinds of questions can feel complicated. You might come back to the same questions over and over, and you may feel surprised by what you discover. You might find that it takes time to find the answers, that your answer changes over time, or that there isn't one.

Grief Playlist

Using music as a guide can help you make sense of big questions. Music lets you feel and express without having to find the words yourself. Try creating a grief playlist.

Instructions

1. Choose songs that remind you of who you were before the person died.

2. Next, choose different songs to describe who you are now.

3. You could also create a separate playlist of songs that help you feel your emotions deeply—the ones that you can cry to, scream to, dance to, or laugh to. You might choose to listen to one of these playlists when you're feeling your grief.

PART IV

Rebuilding a World

Exploring Identity

Grief is like waking up one morning and not knowing

who I am,

where I am,

why I am.

"My grief feels like nothing, like I am numb."

–Anonymous, age 12

Have you ever felt like you're a foreigner inside your own mind? Inside your own body? Inside your own self? Questioning and exploring your identity is a completely normal, but really hard, teen experience. When grief gets added to the mix, it can be even more challenging.

Here's what Ray has to say about exploring their identity after their dad died:

"It's been almost seven years since my dad's death, and I have done a lot of discovering about me and about life. My dad's death gave me more time to focus on myself. That did take a while, though, because at first I was so focused on others, and especially my dad, because that was what I was used to. I still struggle with this today: I'm a big people pleaser. I have had to face a lot of my fears, such as people not liking me if I don't do what they want, along with angry people. I still try to avoid them because they honestly scare the crap out of me. However, I've discovered a lot about myself.

"I'm a queer, trans, nonbinary activist. I love music, taking walks, and learning about people. Everyone is so fascinating. I love listening to people's stories, interests, and adventures, big and small. I still have days, weeks, even months where I feel off. Depression episodes are no joke. That's normal though! Everyone gets them. Even if you fully heal, you will have off days or weeks or months. It's okay to not be okay."

When someone you love dies, you might find you begin a process of unraveling. This is related to asking big questions, but it includes more inner changes. This unraveling happens inside you and might be about the way you think about and view who you are in the world, what makes you special, the kind of person you want to be, how other people see you, and how you want other people to see you. This inner process is often reflected in the actions you take or in the way you think and feel about yourself.

Because it is mostly invisible and because it changes your sense of inner self, the process of unraveling is really difficult. Many teens have told me that it was the hardest part of their grief. Everyone around them—teachers, friends, even their family—saw them as essentially the same person as before the loss. But inside, they knew they had changed.

Some ways that this internal process can take shape externally include:

- taking on traits, likes, or dislikes of the person who died
- trying to "step up" in the family and take on more responsibilities
- attempting to take care of everyone around you

Some ways that this unravelling can affect your internal identity include:

- changes in the values and beliefs you hold about yourself
- seeing the world and other people differently than before
- negative self-talk, guilt, self-blame; *I could have/ should have* language

After this unravelling, you might find that the way you view yourself and your grief and the way others view you are in conflict. You may show your friends and family one side when, internally, you feel something completely different. This is a common experience that both helps and hinders you. It can help by allowing you to get through the day or a tough experience without having to feel your true feelings deeply. However, it can also hinder your ability to know what you are really feeling and to share those feelings with the people who care about you.

Grief Masks

Create a grief mask to show the difference between how you feel about yourself and your grief and how others see you. Finding ways to visualize this difference can provide you with a lot of information about how you are experiencing your grief. It also helps the people in your life see how you are coping with your grief so they can better support you.

Instructions

1. Use a premade blank mask or make your own paper-mache mask.

2. Start on the outside of your mask. Using art materials, choose colors, images, and shapes that that represent what your grief looks like to other people—what you show them.

3. Then, using the same or different materials, create the inside of your mask. Choose colors, images, and shapes that show what your grief looks like on the inside—what you choose to keep or hide from others, what you don't want them to see.

4. When you are finished with your mask, look at it inside and out. Write at least three lines that start with "I am" to create a poem about your grief.

Navigating Friendships and Finding Support

Grief is like finding that the ones you count on don't show up.

And the ones you never knew existed are there, waiting at your door.

—Anonymous

Returning to school, work, and clubs or activities can be some of the hardest experiences after the death of someone you love. When you're grieving, it is often difficult to be around others who aren't also grieving. Friends, teachers, coworkers, and peers may treat you differently, and they may not understand what you're going through. They may have questions you don't want to or can't answer. They may say things that are hurtful, intentionally or unintentionally. They may also surprise you and support you in ways that you never knew they could.

Here is what Ray had to say about returning to school after their dad died by suicide:

"When school started up again, I skipped a lot of it. I mean, I was an eight-year-old kid who had just lost a parent. I'm going to be grieving for a hot minute. I can't even tell you the number of times people came up to me and were like 'OMG, I heard what happened. I'm so sorry!!' And then they'd hug me. I get where they were coming from, and I appreciate it. But being reminded every single day that my dad was dead was draining. On top of that, a lot of people went around talking about it:

"'Did you hear what happened with Ray's dad?'

"'No? What happened?'

"'Get this, their dad killed himself!'

"'What?! No way!'

"And it would all came back to me. Then there were people who said,

"'Ray's dad died ha-ha . . . pass it on!'"

Some of the people in Ray's life were not supportive. In fact, they were hurtful. When someone says or does hurtful things, it can put you in a very hard position. They may be a friend, a coworker, or someone else you see and need to interact with often. But they've also done or said something that hurt you. Some teens find that talking with the person directly is helpful. These conversations don't have to be long or complicated. They can be direct, simple, and offer solutions. For example:

"The other day was my dad's birthday and you didn't say anything to me. I know that you didn't mean to hurt me, but not saying anything was more hurtful. I would rather you bring up my dad and talk about him than not talk about him. Would that be okay for you to do?"

The people around you usually don't intend to hurt you. But when they don't know what to say or do, they may default to doing or saying nothing. In these moments, it's so important to have folks in your life who love you and support you and who you can talk to. And it helps if you can tell these people what you need. Sometimes you might not be sure of what you need. In times like this, keeping communication open and doing your best to verbalize what you think you might need is one way that both you and the people who care for you can support your grief. You can also share information from the Grieving Teens' Bill of Rights (page 131) and What Grieving Teens Want Others to Know (page 133) with your support network as a helpful tool for knowing what you might need.

Support Bracelets

Make a bracelet representing the people in your life who you can go to for support when you need a reminder that you're not alone. For this activity, you'll need at least three different colors of embroidery string or yarn.

Instructions

1. Think of three to five friends and adults you can go to for support. Who can you talk to? Who gets you? Who do you trust when you are feeling your grief? Who listens to you without trying to fix or solve your problems?

2. Think of one color of string to represent each of these people. You should have as many colors of string as people you identified.

3. Then, using those colors, create a bracelet by looping, braiding, or weaving the strings together. Either wear your bracelet or tie it somewhere you'll see it often.

Talking with Others About Your Loss

Grief is like carrying the unimaginable.

Speaking and living the unspoken.

"My grief feels like a bad dream and all I keep doing is screaming."

—Anonymous, age 14

When someone you love dies, your life forever changes. Not just in the day-to-day, but also in how you make new relationships and keep old ones. Have you ever had the experience where you meet someone new who doesn't know your story or anything about your loss and they ask you a question like, *How many siblings do you have?* or *How come you never talk about your mom?* You might be struggling with how to deal with these questions or how to answer them. Or maybe your teachers and friends at school heard about your loss and ask you questions that you aren't ready to answer.

It is always your choice whether you want to share or talk about your loss. On the one hand, if you ignore the answer or make something up that isn't true, you might feel as if you're betraying the memory of your loved one. On the other hand, if you talk about it, then you risk having people say something insensitive or hurtful, or even losing friends.

So, how do you decide what to share and when to share it? These are some strategies teens have used:

"Whatever you choose to tell is okay. You don't owe strangers anything, and they certainly don't have a right to know the most painful parts of your life."

"If you choose not to tell them about your loss, that may be how you protect yourself and the memory of your loved one. New people need to earn your trust."

"If you choose to tell new people about your loss, their reaction says more about them than it does about you or the person you loved. Death makes people uncomfortable, and when people are uncomfortable, they do and say things that can be strange."

"Come up with a script you feel comfortable saying to people."

Grief can feel like it shatters and breaks apart the person you are. As you begin to rebuild and introduce your experiences to new people, you might feel fragmented. How can you visualize these shattered pieces? And how can you put them back together?

Beautifully Broken

The item you use for this activity will need to be broken. Make sure you are okay with intentionally breaking your item, or choose an item that is already broken.

Kintsugi is a Japanese art form loosely translated to mean "golden repair." In kintsugi, broken pottery is mended using lacquer mixed with gold, silver, or platinum. It treats the breakage as part of the pot's history, rather than something to hide. You can create your own piece to symbolize how grief has changed you.

Materials

- something that can be broken, like a pot or cup
- sealable plastic bag
- hot glue or craft glue
- permanent markers
- paints and brushes

Instructions

1. Place your item inside the bag and close the bag tightly.

2. Break the item into a few or many pieces.

3. Carefully remove the pieces and arrange them on a flat surface. Be careful, as some edges may be sharp.

4. Next, use the markers to write messages on the inside or back of the pieces. These messages might be words that remind you of your loved one, memories you have of them, or things you wanted to say to them.

5. Now, carefully glue the pieces back together. Many may not fit perfectly, and that is okay.

6. Once the glue has dried, use the paints to decorate your item in a meaningful way, highlighting the breakage if that feels right to you, or showing how you might explain your grief to someone.

7. Notice how, even if all the pieces can be found and placed back together, the item isn't the same as it was before. How does this process mirror or reflect the way grief has changed you?

PART V

Life After Loss

The New Normal

Grief is like having a piece of me missing forever
and learning how to live with that missing piece.

−Jonah, age 14

IT WON'T EVER BE THE SAME

When someone you love dies, learning how to move forward in your life can be hard. The memories of them live in everything you do and everything you are. The empty chair at the kitchen table, the locker at school unopened, the shoes by the door— reminders are all around.

REFLECT

What do you think about the term "new normal"? Does this fit your experience? If not, what else would you call it?

In the weeks and months after the death, you may find yourself trying to make sense of just how much of your life has changed. This kind of change takes a long time to adjust to. In some ways, you never fully adjust, you just learn to live with this new way of being. Some people call this the "new normal."

This new normal is ongoing and changes over time. In the beginning, it might feel like the new normal is comprised of so many different things: your routine, your friend group, your family structure, and even how you spend holidays. Then, over time, the new normal becomes a part of your everyday life. As with most changes in life, the death of someone we love can make us reflect on how we want to live our lives, what matters most, and even the legacy we want to leave behind. These are all parts of living in this new normal.

Sometimes you might get caught up in the busyness of your everyday life. School, sports, friends, and other responsibilities might take priority. Then, something pulls you out of this routine—maybe a grief burst happens or an anniversary or special date occurs. At those times it can feel unsettling to realize just how much your life may have changed. Some people feel guilty for realizing these changes and others feel deeply sad that this new normal is happening without the person they loved.

In the rush to adjust to a new normal, you may forget to remember how much has changed and how quickly. So many of these changes happen automatically, and everyone who cared about the person may deal with changes in a different way. Some people want to wait before changing things, while others want to change things right away. Taking time to remember and reflect on how much has changed is a normal part of the grieving process. Just like how your grief changes over time, you change too.

 FEEL

Take a moment to reflect on forgetting to remember. What have you forgotten? What do you want to remember? Is there anything you'd like to actively *not* remember, such as fights or experiences that left you feeling upset? How do all these memories feel in your body?

If you have special moments and memories with your loved one and you want to be sure to remember them or you're worried about forgetting them, flip to page 129. The memory jar activity can help you preserve these special memories.

Sometimes thinking about all that has changed—your new normal—can be overwhelming. This is when doing something creative is helpful. The process of creating helps you understand more about your experiences. It can even show those around you just how much has changed for you since the person you love died.

Before/After Collage

A before/after collage is a good way to visually represent all that has changed. Create your collage digitally or make a physical collage using cut-out images, glue, and paper.

Instructions

1. Draw a line directly down the center of your paper or document, so that it looks like the page is cut in half.

2. Label the left side *Before*. Label the right side *After*.

3. Starting on the left, choose images, colors, and words that describe what your life was like before the death.

4. Do the same thing on the right side, depicting what life is like after the death.

5. After you have finished creating your collage, set a timer for three minutes and write whatever comes to mind as you look at your collage.

Celebrating Special Days

Grief is like learning about new parts of myself.
But not having you there to share it with.

"Grief is like being sad all the time but still needing to do things."

—Anonymous, age 12

103

Birthdays, holidays, and special occasions can be really hard when you've lost someone you love. These may be days that were very special for you, days that you shared with your loved one in ways that only the two of you would understand. It may be hard to know how to celebrate those days now. You might feel bad or guilty for wanting to celebrate.

Yet these days are important and should still be special to you. So, how do you keep celebrating these days and honoring your loved one during them? Some teens prefer to include their loved one in private ways that only they know about. Other teens want to include their loved one in more obvious ways.

Ray shares their experience celebrating their dad's birthday and Father's Day:

"My family and I celebrate my dad's birthday, which is March 5, and Father's Day. For my dad's birthday, we usually make a carrot cake or get a pumpkin or apple pie, which were his all-time favorites. We will have a family night, whether that's just dinner together or a game night or we go out. For Father's Day, we kind of do the same thing. A lot of the time, we make crafts or we paint or make collages or something else. We always have fun, that's for sure, and I know my dad has fun watching too."

Whether you choose to celebrate these days publicly, privately, or at all is up to you. If you do wish to celebrate, here are some ideas you might try.

Public:

- Think about how to include your loved one in your celebration in meaningful ways. Did they have a favorite food you can make and enjoy? Did they love a song that you could play? Did they have a favorite holiday tradition you can continue?

- Donate to a charity or not-for-profit organization in their memory.

- Volunteer with a local charity or not-for-profit they supported or whose mission resonated with them.

Private:

- Did they give you something special to wear? Wear it on special days.

- Is there a place you can go to remember your loved one, like a park or other place in your hometown? Go there and spend a few moments remembering the times you shared in that special place.

- Is there a song that is meaningful to you and reminds you of the person? Listen to the song and reflect on the memories you have.

- If you've completed the memory jar activity on page 129, you might celebrate privately by spending time with the special memories you put in your jar.

Finding both public and private ways to honor and remember your loved one might take a little while. Sometimes doing these things will feel really meaningful and other times it might not. That's okay. The things that feel meaningful to you will change over time.

GIVE IT A TRY

Magic Paper Letters

Around holidays and special days, like birthdays, prom, getting your driver's license, or graduating high school, writing a letter to your loved one is a good way to feel connected to them and include them in your celebration.

Instructions

1. Get some water-soluble paper, also known as "magic paper," and fine-tipped markers. You will also need a bowl of water.

2. Using the markers, choose colors that remind you of your loved one and write them a letter. Your letter can be short or long. You can write things you wish you'd said to them or write about how your life has changed.

3. When you are done with the letter, read it out loud or to yourself.

4. Then, submerge the letter in the bowl of water. Watch as the paper dissolves and the ink changes the color of the water.

5. Save the colored water in a jar with a lid that closes tight. Or, if you live by a body of water, you could return the water back to the earth.

Balancing Competing Emotions

Grief is like moving toward fear every single day.

"Grief feels like a wave. If you let it wash over you and don't try to fight it, it will be easier to cope with in the long term."

–Amelie, age 16

Sometimes grief feels all consuming. You might be so overwhelmed by the emotions and the experience that it feels like a bad dream or like nothing at all. It might also feel like holding competing emotions. This is called a duality. A dual emotion is when you feel conflicting—even opposite— emotions at the same time. Dualities might be feeling happy *and* sad, afraid *and* excited, or sorrowful *and* joyful.

Competing emotions in grief can also feel like enjoying yourself for the first time after your loss: laughing and having a good time and then realizing that for just a moment you weren't aware of your grief and the pain you feel. This can be confusing, and some teens have said that they feel guilty for having fun and going on with life.

 INTENTION

Have you ever felt guilty for having fun or going on with life after the person you love died? How do you make sense of the guilt? What helped you (or might help you) work through the guilt so that you could still do fun things and experience life?

Competing emotions can also feel like learning how to hold both the pain and the happiness of a moment. Emotions become more complicated and layered as you grow with your grief. In the beginning it may just be a deep intense sadness. Then, over time, the sadness mixes with joy and hope.

Sofia explains how her grief has changed over time:

"When I first went through the loss of my brother, my grief felt jagged and sharp, like it was a stabbing pain in my chest. It took a long time for that jaggedness to dull and slowly the pain became easier to bear. Most days, grief doesn't affect every little thing I do. Other days it feels heavy, like a big boulder that I'm forced to carry all day. The shapes I could use to describe it are like sharp icicles. But slowly, as we start to bear the pain of the loss and make peace with it, the edges round and they don't feel as painful or sharp. They become more like a rounded triangle."

As you explore and better understand your grief, remember that the goal is not to resolve a conflict in your emotions, but to acknowledge and honor that there is a dual nature to the emotions you experience. Joy and sadness, pain and love can all exist together. The following activity helps you learn how to hold on to dual emotions when thinking about the memories of your loved one.

 REFLECT

Read again what Amelie says about her grief on page 109. What do you think of this? Is it easier in the long run to let your grief "wash over you" or do you think it's easier to fight it? Does this change day to day? How do you think this changes over time?

Sand Memories

To create your sand memories, you'll need the following materials. Note that sand art kits usually have all these. If you don't have sand, try the alternate activity.

- small container with a lid or cap
- small funnel that fits in the container opening
- different colors of sand (6–8 colors is usually enough)
- paper and writing utensil
- Alternate activity materials: different colors of construction paper, glue, and scissors

Instructions

1. Gather your materials and look at your colors of sand. For each color, think of a memory you have with your loved one that you connect to that color. (For

example, one teen I know chose blue and connected it to a memory of a beach vacation with their mom.)

2. On paper, write what each color represents. You should have as many memories as colors of sand.

3. Now, using the funnel, pour the colored sands into your container. You can use however much you want of each color. Some people like to put in equal amounts of each color. Others find that the larger or more meaningful the memory, the more of that color they use.

4. Make sure to tap the container a few times between each color so the sand packs in tightly. Fill to the top and put on the cap or lid.

5. Tie the paper with your written memories around the bottle.

Alternate Activity Instructions

1. Gather your materials and look at your colors of paper. For each color, think of a memory you have with your loved one that you connect to that color.

2. Cut your pieces of paper into any shapes or sizes you like. You could try strips of paper, circles, or hearts.

3. Once you have multiple colors representing multiple memories, glue those shapes onto a new piece of paper.

After you have created your bottle or collage, display it somewhere you can see it often. If you prefer to keep it private, put it somewhere out of sight and take it out whenever you want to look at it. You might use this item when you want to reflect on your memories and emotions.

Continuing the Relationship

Grief is like figuring out that there is nothing to be fixed, nothing that can be fixed.

We learn to carry our grief.

—Anonymous, age 15

Death ends a life, but not the relationship you had with the person. Think about this for a moment.

REFLECT

Do you want to stay connected to your loved one? Why or why not?

This idea can help you reorient the way you think about your loved one. They are not physically present and in your life in the same way, but you can still feel connected to them. Some people like to stay connected to their loved one. Others may feel like that is too weird or doesn't fit with relationship they had with the person. Either way is okay.

Feeling a connection to the person who died is called *continuing bonds*. It means that even though the person is no longer alive, the relationship you have with them continues, if you want it to. Finding moments and experiences throughout your day when you are reminded of the person helps strengthen the connection you feel with them. In turn, a strengthened connection can help you cope with your grief.

Feeling the Connection

A good way to continue a bond with your loved one is to try to infuse their memory and spirit into your everyday life.

Instructions

1. Think of what you loved most about the person who died. Maybe it's a part of their personality or the way they treated other people. Allow those images to fill your memory. What did it feel like to be with your loved one when they were at their best?

2. Now, imagine your loved one as a symbol. This can be a color, something found in nature, a song, anything.

3. What symbol is it? How do you see that symbol in your daily life? How can you add more of it? For example, maybe when you think of the person you see a dragon-fly. You could try to find dragonfly stickers or images and place them around to remind you of the connection.

Conclusion

"At first my grief was heavy, painful, exhausting, unbearable, and I felt angry. But now it's minimal, consistent, transformative, enlightening, empowering, and sometimes recurring."

—Sofia, age 16

Now that you have completed many of the activities in this book, it is helpful to look them over and reflect on where you started and where you are ending.

- When you first picked up this book, did you have any apprehension?
- Were you feeling skeptical?
- How do you feel now?
- How has your understanding of grief changed or evolved after finishing the book?
- How might you come back to the activities in this book in the future and do them again?

Grieving as a teen may be the hardest thing you ever go through. Even though it may feel like you are alone, you aren't. I hope this book, and the activities, quotes, and artwork within, have helped you find the words, shapes, colors, images, and textures to express and describe your grief.

Additional
Activities and Resources

Try these activities and explore the resources on your own or
with others who have experienced a loss. You might even bring
them to your therapist or counselor to work on together.

"My Grief Is Like" Poem and Writing Your Own Analogies

Read the following poem (pages 124–128) about grief. The poem is made up of various analogies about grief, and I wrote it when I started creating this book. After reading the full poem, think about which of its analogies you most connect with (each analogy is one stanza to help you find them quickly). Choose one analogy and then continue to write your own poem from where it leaves off. Or create your own analogies. Add them to your journal.

My Grief Is Like . . .

Someone I love has died.
Someone I love is forever gone.
My world has been shattered.
Turned upside down.
Broken and scattered.
The love I had,
Now makes way for grief.
Grief is like the everlasting shape of that love.

IT'S THE EMOTIONS, THOUGHTS, AND SENSATIONS I FEEL AFTER THE DEATH.

Grief is like a messy
Complex
Layered
All or nothing
Small or large
Ball of yarn

Grief is like an ocean of emotion.
Calm and smooth one moment
The next, a wave appears and knocks me over.

Grief is like having a piece of me missing forever and
learning how to live with that missing piece.

Grief is like a pounding in the chest, an aching in the muscles, and a
breaking of the heart.

Why do I feel so tired all the time?

GRIEF IS LIKE WAKING UP ONE MORNING AND NOT KNOWING
WHO I AM,
WHERE I AM,
WHY I AM.

Grief is like learning to question,
unlearn,
and relearn the world around me.
Who am I now?
What will I become?

Grief is like learning about new parts of myself.
But not having you there to share it with

Grief is like walking through a thick fog, but the fog is in
my brain.

Grief is like finding that the ones you count on don't show up.
And the ones you never knew existed are there, waiting at your door.

GRIEF IS LIKE CARRYING THE UNIMAGINABLE.
SPEAKING AND LIVING THE UNSPOKEN.

Grief is like moving toward fear every single day.

**Grief is like holding on and letting go at the same time.
It is finding ways to remember and build new memories.**

*Grief is like living in an altered reality.
Two realties at once.
The reality that my loved one is gone
And
The reality that everyone else seems to have moved on.
I'm still in the reality where I can't believe you're gone.*

Grief is like figuring out that there is nothing to be fixed, nothing that
can be fixed.
We learn to carry our grief.

GRIEF IS LIKE . . .

Grief is like a fear that crept in overnight.
Took up residence and won't move its suitcase.
I keep tripping over it each time I walk in the house.

Grief is like the static on an old television.
It's always there.
Sometimes you see it, and other times you don't.

Grief is like celebrating the milestones, the happy moments,
the joy of life
and honoring the missing pieces of you scattered in the wind.

Grief is like my body has transformed into something unknown.
There is an emptiness that is indescribable.
It gnaws away, like an itch that can't be scratched.

Grief is like the subtle way that everyone tries to not
say their name for fear
that will 'remind me' of you.
I will always be reminded.
Please, say their name.

GRIEF IS LIKE A POEM WITHOUT AN ENDING.

Memory Jar

You might worry about forgetting your loved one or about not having many memories of them in the first place. One way to hold onto and honor memories of your loved one is to create a memory jar.

Materials

- clear jar with a lid
- colored tissue paper
- decoupage glue
- paper
- battery-powered candle

Instructions

1. Using the tissue paper and glue, decorate the outside of the jar in colors that remind you of the person who died.

2. Now, on small slips of paper, write down memories of the person that are special to you and place them inside the jar.

3. Once you have all the memories you want in the jar, place the battery-powered candle inside and turn it on.

Your jar should light up, showing the colors you used to decorate, and be filled on the inside with those special memories. You can turn on the candle whenever you are feeling close to your loved one, when you want to take out and read the memories, or even when you just want to see the colors and think of the person.

Grieving Teens' Bill of Rights

This Bill of Rights was created by teens at Dougy Center for teens who are grieving. You might use it as a reminder to yourself or share with trusted adults or friends as a helpful tool for what you might be needing in your grief.

As grieving teens, we have the right to:

- know the truth about the death, the person who died, and the circumstances surrounding the death
- ask questions and have them answered honestly
- be heard and listened to without receiving unsolicited advice
- be silent and not share our thoughts and emotions out loud
- disagree with your perceptions and conclusions
- see the person who died and the place where they died, if we choose to
- grieve in our own ways—without hurting ourselves or others
- feel all the feelings and think all the thoughts of our own unique grief

- not have to follow the "Stages of Grief" as outlined in a high school health book
- be angry at death, the person who died, God, ourselves, and others
- disagree with people who are insensitive, especially those who spout clichés
- have our own beliefs about life and death
- be involved in the decisions about the rituals related to the death
- have irrational guilt about what we could have done to prevent the death

What Grieving Teens Want Others to Know

You may be feeling very alone in your grief and wish that your parents and other adults in your life knew how to better support you. Below are some things teens have shared that they wished their parents knew. Read through this list and notice which ones you resonate with. Then, make your own list. When you are finished with your list, think about who you would like to share it with and when.

- Even though I might not be crying, I'm still hurting.
- Even though I don't talk to you, it doesn't mean I don't want to be asked.
- Even if I'm alone in my room, I still want you to come check on me.
- Even though it looks like I'm fine and together, I'm falling apart inside.
- Even though you don't cry in front of me to protect me, I do the same for you
- Ask me what I think and what I want to do, even if I shrug and don't respond.
- Keep saying their name and telling me when you miss them.

Organizations & Websites

Dougy Center (dougy.org). Dougy Center is a nonprofit organization that has been dedicated to supporting grieving children, teens, and families since 1982. They have free resources online, provide training to teachers and counselors, and offer support groups at their location in Portland, Oregon.

What's Your Grief (whatsyourgrief.com). What's Your Grief is a website that provides free resources and blog posts for anyone grieving a loss. Their content is easy to read and short, providing accurate and helpful tips on grief and stories about loss.

National Alliance for Children's Grief (nacg.org). The National Alliance for Children's Grief is a national organization dedicated to advancing research on childhood grief and loss. They host an annual conference for professionals to present their work and also provide grants so that community organizations can offer free grief support.

Camp Erin (elunanetwork.org/camps-programs/camp-erin). Camp Erin is the largest national bereavement program for youth and families grieving the death of a significant person in their lives. Check out the website to see if there is a Camp Erin near you.

Index

About the Author

With training as a child life specialist and thanatologist, Dr. Korie Leigh has spent over twenty years specializing in working with children and families experiencing grief and loss. As an associate professor and program director, she teaches graduate courses on child development, death, dying, and bereavement.

Dr. Leigh obtained her Ph.D. in transpersonal psychology, where she wrote her dissertation on the lived experiences of bereaved parents. She also holds an M.A. in public health and grief counseling and a B.A. in child development. She speaks and presents at national and regional conferences on issues of grief, loss, and coping. She is also the author of *What Does Grief Feel Like?*, a picture book for children. She lives in Santa Fe, New Mexico.